Takes Me Camping

BY:
AJ NICHOLLS

To the man who was always there for me, taught me everything I know.

From the good times around the pool table, to the countless hours in the shop.

You have impacted everybody's life in our family and I am so grateful to call you my Papa.

I have created this Papa John series so I can pass all the knowledge that you gave me, onto other little ones who weren't quite as lucky as I was.

I Love You Papa
And
Thank-You for Everything.

Today, Papa John and I are going camping for the first time. I have never been camping before, but Papa John said that camping is fun, and we get to sleep in his big trailer and go fishing since I now know how to.

He said that we're going to have campfires and cook marshmallows. Then he would pull out his guitar and sing songs. It sounds like so much fun!

But, Papa said we need to pack a lot of things into his big camper to go camping.

We need to pack our clothes, bedding, flashlights, fishing gear, chairs, and firewood. Papa and I went and gathered all the things that we needed, we put them into his big camper and we headed for the campground.

"Are you ready to do some fun camping?" Papa asked. "I'm excited!" I said.

The campground was really far away, so Papa and I had to drive for so long, and I got so bored sitting in the back of the truck. Just when I was about to ask Papa, "are we there yet," we pulled into the campground.

Once we got to our campsite,
we had to pick the perfect spot
to set up the camper.
"Should we leave it here bud,
or move it over there?"
Papa asked.
"I like it where it's at Papa," I
said eager to set everything up.

We unhooked the truck and leveled the trailer. Then we set up the awning and started to unload the firewood from the back of the truck.

There was a lot of firewood
and it was heavy, so Papa
helped me.

We got all the firewood out
and unpacked our fishing gear.

Papa and I then went into the camper and made our beds so they would be ready for us later that night.
Everything was ready!

"Now, let the fun begin! Let's go down to the lake." Papa said as he grabbed our fishing gear, and we headed down to the lake.

"Do you remember how to do this buddy?" Papa asked. "I had so much fun the first time, how could I forget Papa!" I replied. Papa helped me get my fishing pole ready, and I cast it into the lake. Papa watched proudly with a smile on his face. He grabbed his fishing pole and cast it in as well.

We had a lot of fun sitting on the shore fishing even though we didn't catch any fish. But Papa told me stories, like how he met grandma in a pickle factory!

"Well, my Boy, do you want to go back to the camper, get changed and go swimming?" Papa asked.

"That sounds awesome Papa!" I replied excitedly!

So we packed up our fishing gear and walked back to the campsite. Papa and I got changed into our swimsuits. We grabbed our towels, and off we went to the pool.

The pool had a lot of people there and the water was cold! "The water is too cold for me Papa." I told him.

"That's ok bud, you have to get used to it. Come with me and we will go in together." Papa replied.

Papa and I slowly walked into the water until, before i knew it, we were all the way in!

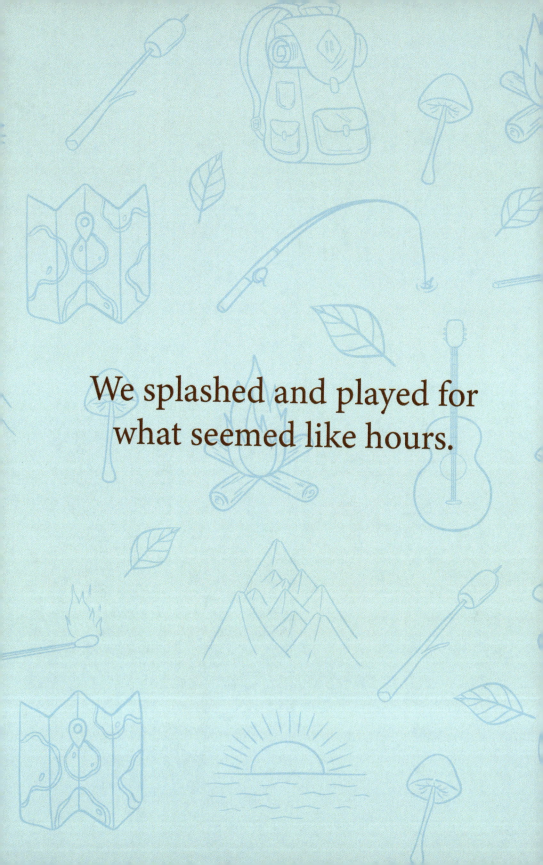

We splashed and played for
what seemed like hours.

After swimming, Papa and I went back to the campsite to eat supper.
Papa packed us some hot dogs, so we found some big sticks and cooked hot dogs over the open fire.

After we ate and filled our bellies, Papa built the campfire up higher by adding more wood.

Sitting by the fire, I asked
Papa, "Can you play the
guitar?"
"Well, I can try," Papa said
with a big smile on his face.
Papa got out his guitar and sat
back down by the campfire.
He cleared his throat a couple
times, looked at me and said,
"Watch this!"

I just laughed at him as he started playing songs that I have never even heard of before that night.

"This is 'Beat the Cheat out of you' by Pinkard & Bowden." Papa started playing and singing.

"Pretty good, eh!" Papa impressed himself.

"Here's The Ring of Fire by Johnny Cash."

Papa was playing and singing things from way before I was born. I had no idea what he was singing, but I was laughing, he was happy and that made it a good night!

Papa stopped singing and was just playing and humming. I was looking up at the stars listening to Papa, and I started to yawn.

"Getting tired, my Boy?" Papa asked.

"I am getting there Papa." I replied.

So he kept playing and humming, but it didn't take long for me to become very tired.
"Looks like it's time for bed," Papa said, and we went into the big camper.
I had a great time with Papa on my first camping trip. I had a lot of fun and enjoyed every minute. I hope Papa and I could go camping together again soon.

Thank You Papa!